BECOMING AN EFFECTIVE TUTOR

Lynda B. Myers

CRISP PUBLICATIONS, INC.
Los Altos, California

BECOMING AN EFFECTIVE TUTOR

Lynda B. Myers

CREDITS
Editor: **W. Philip Gerould**
Designer: **Carol Harris**
Typesetting: **Interface Studio**
Cover Design: **Carol Harris**
Artwork: **Ralph Mapson**

Copyright © 1990 by Crisp Publications, Inc.
Printed in the United States of America

English language Crisp books are distributed worldwide. Our major international distributors include:

CANADA: Reid Publishing, LTD., Box 7267, Oakville, Ontario Canada L6J 6L6. TEL: (416) 842-4428, FAX: (416) 842-9327

AUSTRALIA: Career Builders, P. O. Box 1051, Springwood, Brisbane, Queensland, Australia 4127. TEL: 841-1061, FAX: 841-1580

NEW ZEALAND: Career Builders, P. O. Box 571, Manurewa, Auckland, New Zealand. TEL: 266-5276, FAX: 266-4152

JAPAN: Phoenix Associates Co., Mizuho Bldg. 2-12-2, Kami Osaki, Shinagawa-Ku, Tokyo 141, Japan. TEL: 3-443-7231, FAX: 3-443-7640

Selected Crisp titles are also available in other languages. Contact International Rights Manager Tim Polk at (415) 949-4888 for more information.

Library of Congress Catalog Card Number 89-82096
Myers, Lynda B.
Becoming An Effective Tutor
ISBN 1-56052-028-0

Introduction to Tutoring

Why should I be a tutor?

As a tutor you will share your knowledge, your skills, your time, your talents, your highest and best self with a total stranger. At times you will feel frustrated, discouraged, exasperated, exhausted, confused. At other times you will feel triumphant, confident, joyful, energetic, brilliant. As a tutor you may expect to give, but you may be surprised to find that you also receive in great abundance. You may earn a few dollars, keep current in a subject, gain deeper insights, discover new resources, make a new friend. Tutoring is sharing yourself with another student in a way that makes a difference in both your lives.

What does a tutor do?

Tutors are students who have specific knowledge or skills to share with other students. Tutors are selected by a process which varies, but usually includes an application, interviews, and instructor approval. Once tutors are accepted they meet with individuals or small groups on a regular basis to clarify problems and upgrade study skills. Tutor and tutee might review class material, discuss the text, predict test questions, formulate ideas for a paper, or work on solutions to problems. But what tutors do best is inspire other students to succeed.

What about my own studies?

Tutors are good students, and they are valuable in this helping role because they *are* good students. Tutors are expected to plan their schedules so that they have the time and energy to keep up their own grades. Many students find that tutoring actually improves their grades because it helps to keep them current in their field. Students who tutor often improve their own study habits, besides improving their reading, writing, and communication skills as they learn new ways to assist others.

Are there any other benefits?

Tutoring provides valuable experience related to many fields, including business, teaching, and health care. Tutoring experience looks good on a resumé and sounds good in an interview. Tutoring experience COUNTS!

How will I know what to do?

The following lessons are designed to help you develop your personal strengths so that you can become a competent, effective tutor.

To Pam

"Sometimes I think the things we see are shadows of the things to be;
That what we plan we build..."

Phoebe Cary, "Dreams, Realities", St.7.

"Our work brings us face to face with love."

Mother Teresa

CONTENTS

UNIT 1

GETTING STARTED

LESSON 1: FORMING AN INTENTION

OBJECTIVE

In this lesson you will have the opportunity to form a firm intention about tutoring other students.

PRACTICE

Complete the Intention Exercise near the end of the lesson.

How to Form an Intention That Leads to Success

Forming an intention means creating the circumstances for something to happen and making a commitment to see it through, *no matter what.* An intention with regard to tutoring means a commitment to playing a positive role in another person's academic life and a willingness to be accountable for that person's success.

Committing ourselves means:

1. We will be dependable. We will show up for tutoring sessions.
2. We will be prepared for the sessions both academically and emotionally. We will be ready to focus our attention on the needs of the student.

Being accountable means that we accept responsibility for our part in our student's success. It does not mean usurping the student's responsibility for herself or himself—it means doing whatever we can to keep the person on track.

We form an intention because we expect some reward even though there may be a price to pay.

A *reward* is some good that we expect as a result of our efforts. For tutors some rewards might be:

1. Increased self-respect
2. Increased confidence
3. Pleasure in helping another person succeed
4. Some extra money
5. Job experience
6. Increased knowledge of the subject matter

A *price* is whatever it costs to get the job done. Some prices we are willing to pay; some prices we are not.

For tutors some acceptable prices might be:

1. Less free time
2. Less time available for other work
3. Less time to watch TV
4. The possibility that I will find tutoring is not for me

Unacceptable prices might be:

1. Less time for one's own studies
2. Lower grades
3. Family problems

The rewards must be worth the prices.

Intention Exercise

Take a few minutes now to consider the rewards that you expect to receive from tutoring and the prices that you are willing to pay for those rewards.

REWARDS I expect: _____

_____

_____

PRICES I am willing to pay: _____

_____

PRICES I am not willing to pay: _____

_____

Now that you have considered the rewards and possible prices of tutoring, you are ready to complete the tutor's intention statement below.

Tutor's Intention Statement

My intention for this term is to assist _____ other students in the following course(s):

_____

I will help them to understand the material, to stay enrolled, and to earn better grades.

_____

I will know that I have succeeded when: _____

_____

Keeping the intention of the whole term in mind, commit yourself to carrying it out each day. Complete the following statement now and each time that you tutor a student:

My intention for today is: _____

LESSON 2: WORKING WITH AN INSTRUCTOR

OBJECTIVES

In this lesson you will have the opportunity to:
1. Initiate contact with an instructor.
2. Maintain contact throughout the term.
3. Ask questions that will help you in tutoring.

PRACTICE

Complete the Tutor's Report at the end of the lesson.

How to Work with an Instructor

Tutoring involves a close working relationship with the instructor of the student being assisted. A tutor is expected to initiate contact with the instructor before tutoring begins and to contact the instructor at least once a month for the rest of the term.

How do I contact an instructor?

Most instructors have an office on campus. The office hours are usually posted near the office door. Phone during an office hour to make an appointment. The first visit should be a 30-minute appointment. Some instructors may be hard to reach, so it is best to go to the class to meet them and make an appointment to talk later.

What do I say?

On the first visit explain that you want to be a tutor for the instructor's class. Discuss the background that qualifies you to do that. Ask for a course syllabus, a reading list, a class calendar, and, if possible, a copy of the text. Ask to visit the class to introduce yourself as the tutor so that students will know you are available. Also ask for any advice that the instructor might have for you. Plan to meet again in about a month for 10-15 minutes.

How to Work with an Instructor (Continued)

On subsequent visits ask questions such as the following—even if you think you already know the answers. The instructor's responses might surprise you.

1. Has my tutee been attending class?
2. Has she or he been completing homework assignments?
3. How can I best help her or him succeed in your class?
4. Can you suggest any additional materials for her or him?
5. Have you noticed any improvement since I have been tutoring her or him?
6. Do you have any advice for me?
7. I would like to meet regularly to check on my tutee's progress. Could we make an appointment for next month now?

Tutor's Report

The courses that I intend to tutor this semester are:

_____

_____

_____

_____

The instructors whose students I intend to tutor this semester are:

Name:	Office Hours:	Phone Number:	Approved? (Y/N)
_____	_____	_____	_____
_____	_____	_____	_____
_____	_____	_____	_____
_____	_____	_____	_____

LESSON 3: COACHING TUTEES TO WIN

OBJECTIVE

> In this lesson you will have the opportunity to become a competent coach for your tutee.

PRACTICE

> Complete the Coaching Practice at the end of the lesson.

How to Coach Tutees to Win

Competent tutors have a winning game plan. No matter what the subject, a winning game plan includes these FIVE STEPS TO SUCCESS:

1. **Assessment**
2. **Demonstration**
3. **Practice**
4. **Feedback**
5. **Positive messages**

ASSESSMENT

Assessment means finding out where to begin. You do not usually need a special test for this in tutoring. When you meet with the student for the first time, ask him or her what help is needed. However, many students do not really know what help they need, so you must look for other clues as well.

1. Talk to the tutee's instructor (see Lesson 2).
2. Ask to look at some written work associated with the class.
3. Ask the student whether he or she has been attending class.

Written work may give you an idea of the student's strengths and weaknesses in the subject. If you need help interpreting the written work, check with the instructor. Missed classes and incomplete homework are danger signs. They may indicate that the student lacks a serious intention with regard to the course. Talk to the student about his or her attitude. You may find it helpful to use the materials in Lesson 1 of this book. If you need further direction, see the tutee's instructor.

How to Coach Tutees to Win (Continued)

Assessment does not need to be completed before you begin tutoring. It can be a process that takes part of several sessions. For best results, assume that your student knows *nothing* about the subject until she or he has demonstrated otherwise.

DEMONSTRATION

Demonstration involves showing as well as telling the student what to do. This is an important point, since most of us who tutor love to hear the sound of our own voice. Unfortunately for us, most people will not be enlightened by our words alone. We must *show* our students what we mean.

We might work a sample problem, explaining the steps as we go. We might draw a diagram, make a chart, or write notes. The important thing is to illustrate the problem-solving process for the student. In this way we provide the student with two sources of information: auditory (your words) and visual (your actions). By inviting the student to participate—for example by working sample problems— you add a third source of information, kinesthetic (the student's actions).

When we present information using all three learning modalities—auditory, visual, and kinesthetic—we significantly help our students to get what we are saying. If they do not understand our auditory explanation, the visual diagram may make it clear, or they may grasp the idea as they participate in the kinesthetic problem-solving process. Showing as well as telling gets our students *involved* from the very start.

PRACTICE

Practice is the step that puts the tutor's patience to the test. As our student practices the material he or she may be tentative and clumsy. At this point most of us are eager to rush in and correct the mistakes. No matter how well meaning, our assistance at this point can only interfere with the student's learning.

Our silent encouragement is what the student needs most as she struggles with the material on her own. If she runs into difficulty we wait—for at least 15 seconds!—until she has had a chance to think it through.

FEEDBACK

Feedback provides the student with important, specific information about the practice exercise. Both positive and negative feedback are necessary, important, and desired by the serious student. Of course everyone enjoys basking in the joy of positive feedback: "That's right!" "Yes!" "Good job!" However, negative feedback is perhaps even more valuable. It limits our mistakes and guides us back to the right track.

Negative feedback need not be threatening to a student ("Not like that! There you go again."). Words that express disapproval can undermine a person's confidence and may lead to failure.

Negative feedback that encourages may sound something like this: "This doesn't sound quite right. Could you say (or do) it another way?" "You set up the equation correctly. Let's see what happened after that . . ."

Specific feedback focuses on the problem, not the person. For example: "This sentence seems vague to me. What are you really trying to say here?" "There is a mistake in this solution. Do you see it?"

Feedback is an important part of the tutor/student relationship. Both positive and negative feedback are useful, but the tutor must be careful to direct negative feedback to the specific problem, not the person, and to use words that encourage rather than discourage.

How to Coach Tutees to Win (Continued)

POSITIVE MESSAGES

Like the coach who sends a team out to the playing field with a hearty "Go for it!" an effective tutor affirms the student's highest goals by ending tutoring sessions with a positive message. Statements like these, when given from the heart, can make a real difference in another person's performance: "You will remember everything you need to know." "You will concentrate easily." "You are a capable, competent writer." "You will complete the assignment with ease."

By the end of the session, you will know what your tutee needs to hear from you. Say it to him or her and dare to inspire success.

Remember that you, the tutor, deserve positive messages too. Nourish yourself with these self-affirming messages, or make up your own:

> I am a powerful, loving, giving person.
> I am a capable, competent, mature adult.
> I am worthy and deserving.
> I have everything I need to be successful.
> Wherever I go I am valued and admired.

Competent tutoring means having a successful game plan that includes assessment, demonstration, practice, feedback, and positive messages. Competent tutoring means coaching your tutee to win.

Coaching Practice

Develop a winning game plan for a student you are tutoring.

1. Three questions I can use for assessment:

   1) _____

   2) _____

   3) _____

2. Three examples of demonstrations I may use to show as well as tell my tutee what to do:

   1) _____

   2) _____

   3) _____

3. Negative feedback requires tact and practice. Three examples of the ways I plan to give negative feedback are:

   1) _____

   2) _____

   3) _____

4. Two positive messages that will affirm my tutee's highest goals and best intentions are:

   1) _____

   2) _____

5. Two positive messages that will affirm my own highest goals and best intentions:

   1) _____

   2) _____

LESSON 4: ORGANIZING A TUTORING SESSION

OBJECTIVES

> **In this lesson you will have an opportunity to:**
> 1. **Prepare for a tutoring session.**
> 2. **Plan the session in advance.**
> 3. **Evaluate the session afterwards.**
>
> **You will also learn about group tutoring.**

PRACTICE

> 1. **Complete the Tutor's Intention Worksheet before a tutoring session.**
> 2. **Complete the Tutoring Session Plan before the same session.**
> 3. **Complete the Tutor's Evaluation after the tutoring session.**

How to Organize a Tutoring Session

The Tutor's Intention Worksheet prepares you to plan a tutoring session based on total commitment, as practiced in Lesson 1.

This is followed by the Tutoring Session Plan, a step-by-step guide to preparing for a meeting with a tutee. This guide is based on the winning game plan covered in Lesson 3.

Keep your intention in mind as you complete the Tutoring Session Plan. Think carefully about your responses to each section. There are no right or wrong answers, but your plan should show your ability to be well organized yet flexible.

The Tutor's Evaluation at the end of the session allows you to savor the successes of the session and to think about possible improvements for next time.

You may wish to make photocopies of these forms to use regularly with your tutoring sessions.

14

Tutor's Intention Worksheet

Tutor _____ Subject _____

Date _____ Time _____ Place _____

Name(s) of your Tutees(s): _____

1. Complete this tutor's intention statement:

   My intention for today is _____

   _____

   _____

2. Use a scale of 0 (lowest) to 10 (highest) for the following items:

   My level of involvement in this session will be _____ .

   My tutee's level of involvement in this session will be _____ .

   My preparation for this session is _____ .

   The way I feel about this tutoring session is _____ .

3. A positive message I can give myself right now is:

   _____

4. A positive message I can give my tutee today is:

   _____

Tutoring Session Plan

Tutor _____ Subject _____

Date _____ Time _____ Place _____

Name(s) of your Tutees(s): _____

1. What do you plan to cover in this session?

   _____

2. How do you plan to assess your student's needs today?

   _____

3. How do you plan to demonstrate what you expect the student to do?

   _____

4. What will you say or do to give positive feedback when the student does well?

   _____

5. What will you say or do to give negative feedback when necessary?

   _____

6. If a problem arises, or if you have a question, what will you do?

   _____

7. What will you do or say if the tutee is late?

   _____

8. What will you do if the tutee does not come at all?

   _____

9. How will you decide when to meet again?

   _____

10. How will you decide what to cover next time?

    _____

11. What do you expect the tutee to do to prepare for the next session?

    _____

12. How will you let the tutee know what you expect her or him to do to prepare for next time?

    _____

13. How will you prepare for the next session?

    _____

14. How will you and the tutee get in touch if one of you cannot attend the next session? (Give three alternatives if possible.)

    _____

    or _____

    or _____

Tutoring Session Evaluation

Complete the following statements:

1. What I did well today was _____

2. What I need to improve is _____

3. What my tutee did well today was _____

4. What my tutee needs to improve is _____

5. Plans for next time:

   Time and place of next meeting: _____

   Material to be covered _____

   Tutor's preparation _____

   Tutee's preparation _____

   If one of us cannot be there, he or she will

   _____

   or _____

   or _____

Group Tutoring

For various practical reasons many tutors work with groups of students rather than with one person at a time. While groups may be efficient in terms of resources, they do present some special challenges for tutors. The following information may help you organize effective tutoring groups.

Groups ideally include between three and five students enrolled in the same class. If the group is larger, it may be helpful to form partnerships of two or three students who work together and help each other. The term *collaborative learning* is frequently used to refer to this type of group process.

Ground rules for participation in the tutoring group establish common expectations among all participants. For example, the students in the group may agree to assist each other and to ask for help if they need it. A group tutoring contract, such as the one at the end of this section, may assist you to establish ground rules for your tutoring group.

Two ground rules are especially important for tutoring groups:

1. that students agree to attempt the assignment on their own before the meeting, and

2. that students agree to come to the session with questions prepared.

Without this structure the tutoring session may become limited to a review of the lecture or the book, while difficulties in understanding persist. Often several students will have the same questions, and this makes a good place to start the session.

Group members should be encouraged to answer questions for each other when possible. Explaining the information to someone else both reinforces the material and raises the self-esteem of the person sharing. When group members share the responsibility for generating and answering questions, the focus becomes one of group inquiry rather than one of group helplessness. This raises the self-esteem of the whole group.

Group tutoring can be a positive experience for all concerned. The tutees often appreciate discovering that they are not the only ones with questions. Most tutees enjoy the opportunity for helping others, as well as receiving help.

Most tutors enjoy working with groups because they can serve more students in less time, because they are not solely responsible for assisting with every problem, and because tutoring groups are fun. Many tutors find that their groups accomplish more than the students who are individually tutored.

Group Tutoring Contract

I am a member of the Tutoring Group for the _____ class.

I agree to follow these ground rules:

1. I will arrive on time and ready to work.
2. I will attempt the homework ahead of time.
3. I will come with questions prepared.
4. I will ask for help when I need it.
5. I will assist others in the group whenever I can, since explaining the material to another person helps me as well.
6. I will attend class regularly.
7. I will not use the tutoring session to find out what happened in any class I missed. Instead I will make arrangements to borrow someone's notes on my own.
8. I will give positive messages to others as often as possible.
9. I will accept positive messages from others.
10. I will not give negative messages, nor will I accept them from others.

Signed _____

Witnessed by _____

U N I T 2

COMMUNICATION

Secretaries have typewriters, doctors have stethoscopes, housekeepers have brooms. The tools of the trade for tutors are effective speaking and active listening. These skills allow information to flow freely between people. They make a tutoring relationship work.

Lesson 5 discusses effective speaking—how to speak so that people listen. Lesson 6 will discuss active listening—how to listen so that you really hear.

LESSON 5: EFFECTIVE SPEAKING

OBJECTIVES

> In this lesson you will have the opportunity to learn and practice five steps to effective speaking. These five steps will enable you to speak so that people listen.

PRACTICE

> 1. Complete the Effective Speaking Practice.
> 2. Complete the Effective Speaking Evaluation at the end of the lesson.

How to Speak so That People Will Listen

''Listen!'' ''You're not listening!'' ''No one ever listens to me!'' Almost everyone has had the experience of saying something important and not being heard. For a tutor this can be a serious problem. The student *must* hear the tutor, for the tutor is often the last hope. How can a tutor speak in such a compelling way that people listen? Here's a method that works:

The five steps to effective speaking:

1. **Prepare yourself**
2. **Prepare the listener**
3. **Say it!**
4. **Make a contract**
5. **Appreciate the listener (and yourself)**

5 Steps to Effective Speaking

Prepare Yourself

Effective speaking begins when we decide that we have something important to say. Most people never say the things that they really want to say because they do not know how. Or because they are afraid. Or, often, because they do not know what they want to say.

How can we know what it is that we want to say to another person? Right now, call to mind an important person in your life. Imagine that person standing in front of you. Take a few minutes to think about what you would like to say to that person.

You may find yourself feeling strongly about the things you want to say. You may feel mad or sad or afraid. These feelings are a sure sign that you have something important to say. Let your feelings guide you as you write down your thoughts:

What I want is _____

What I resent is _____

What I need from you is _____

I am afraid that _____

What I appreciate about you is _____

The way I want our relationship to be is _____

Prepare the Listener

Once we know what we want to say, we must get the listener's attention. If we simply begin talking, as we often do, the other person probably won't attach much importance to what we are saying. Often we get people's attention with anger or threats: ''Did you leave this mess?'' ''Who took my pen?'' This puts the other person on the defensive—''I didn't do it!''—rather than enlisting his or her cooperation.

A better way to get a person's attention is to ask directly for what we want. For example: ''I need to discuss a problem with you. Can we talk now?'' If the other person is not available at that moment, arrange another time that is mutually acceptable: ''I have to leave right now. Could we talk later? Say, four o'clock? Yes, I'll see you at four.''

Say It!

Once you have the person's attention you can keep it by asking directly for what you want. This may be uncomfortable. Many of us are used to hinting and hoping other people will guess what we want (and give it to us without too much fuss). If we ask directly for what we want there are risks. We might be turned down. We might be embarrassed, insulted, or blamed. On the other hand, we might get what we want.

Since we have not had much luck with hinting, we might decide to risk some discomfort, just for today, by asking directly for what we want. Like this: ''I want to talk about our meeting times. I'm not comfortable planning to meet at nine o'clock and then not getting started until almost 9:30.'' Try it:

I want to talk about _____

_____

_____

As you speak, be congruent. Keep your body posture and expression consistent with what you are saying. If this matter is important to you, let it show—in your body, on your face, in your eyes! *Say* what you want and *look* like you mean it.

Perhaps what you want involves a behavior change for another person. You may be fed up with his arriving late, not showing up, or not being prepared. However, it is important not to threaten the person with shouts and angry words. A person who feels threatened concentrates on defending herself rather than on cooperating.

Statements which begin with the word ''you'' tend to sound threatening, as in: ''You always . . .'' ''You never . . .'' ''Why can't you ever . . .''

Statements which begin with the word ''I'' are more effective. They tell the other person what you feel without accusing or blaming. For example: ''I feel upset when you are late and you don't call.'' ''I feel angry when I come here on time and you don't show up.'' These statements follow a pattern that is easy to remember: I feel _____ when _____ (happens).

Try this pattern now with a statement that you want to make:

I feel _____ when _____

Imagine yourself making this statement, then waiting for the other person to respond. Imagine what he or she would say. Perhaps the response would be: ''I'm sorry,'' followed by an excuse. Perhaps the response would be angry or sad. The active listening technique described in the next chapter will help you deal with the other person's reaction.

Make a Contract

Before ending the discussion, ask the other person to make a contract with you about how this situation will be in the future: ''Do you agree to phone if you can't make it?'' ''Yes, if I can, otherwise I will ask someone else to phone for me.''

Appreciate the Other Person

As a last step, appreciate the other person: ''Thanks for listening,'' ''Thanks for talking with me about this,'' ''I'm glad we talked.''

Effective Speaking Practice

1. Choose an unfinished situation in your life right now. Decide on one important message that you want to share with someone involved in that situation.

   Who is the person _____

   What do you want to say _____

2. Write four ways to ask that person directly for something you want.

   1. _____
   2. _____
   3. _____
   4. _____

3. Write five ''I'' statements that you might say to that person.

   1. _____
   2. _____
   3. _____
   4. _____
   5. _____

4. Suggest three possible contracts that you would be willing to make with that person.

   1. _____
   2. _____
   3. _____

5. Suggest three statements to appreciate that person.

   1. _____
   2. _____
   3. _____

6. Suggest three statements to appreciate yourself.

   1. _____
   2. _____
   3. _____

Effective Speaking Evaluation

1. Did you share the important message that you wrote at the beginning of the Effective Speaking Practice?   Yes _____   No _____

2. If yes, explain briefly what happened. If no, explain briefly why not.

_____

_____

_____

3. How did you ask for what you wanted?

_____

_____

_____

4. What "I" statements did you use?

_____

_____

_____

5. What contract did you agree on?

_____

_____

_____

6. How did you appreciate the other person?

_____

_____

_____

7. How did you appreciate yourself?

_____

_____

_____

LESSON 6: ACTIVE LISTENING

OBJECTIVES

In this lesson you will have the opportunity to:
1. Find out what is meant by "active listening."
2. Practice using active listening.
3. Reflect on the ways that active listening makes a difference in your relationships.

PRACTICE

1. Do the Active Listening Practice with given statements.
2. Do the Active Listening Practice with people in your life.
3. Notice how active listening makes a difference in your relationships.

How to Listen so That You Really Hear

Active listening helps us to really hear other people not to hear what we expect them to say, or what we want them to say, or what we ourselves are getting ready to say. It helps us truly to hear what the other person is in fact saying to us. In active listening, sometimes called "reflective listening," we summarize what the speaker has said.

For example, a student might say to us: "Sorry I'm late today. The kids let the dog out and we had to go find him, and then a friend called and wouldn't get off the phone, then my car wouldn't start, and besides I have a splitting headache." There are many possible responses to this sort of statement, all the way from "It doesn't matter" to advice about latches, time management, or headaches.

A better response would be a simple summary, without giving advice and without excusing the inconvenience. For example: "Sounds like you've had a terrible morning!" This response reflects what the other person said, period. It is not critical, evaluative, or guilt provoking. It does not provide advice that may not be wanted, and it does not excuse the person for being late.

Active Listening (Continued)

Active listening leaves the responsibility for what has been said *with the speaker*. In other words, the active listener assumes that the speaker can solve his or her own problems. The active listener cares about the speaker but does not become involved in the problem. For example:

Speaker: I'm out of money until payday.
Active Listener: Broke, huh?

Notice that the active listener did not offer to loan the person money, nor did she commiserate with the speaker by saying something like, "Oh, you poor thing." What she did do was to reflect what she heard, leaving responsibility for the situation with the speaker.

Isn't this hard-hearted, you may say? No, it is not. By allowing other people to own their own problems, we indicate faith in their ability to resolve them. When we rush in with advice and solutions we imply that the other person is less competent to solve problems than we are.

How would you, as the speaker, feel when confronted by these responses?

Speaker: I forgot my book.

"You'd better go home and get it. You *must* get this assignment finished today."
Competent _____ Incompetent _____

"How awful! No book! You will never get the assignment finished now!"
Competent _____ Incompetent _____

"Well, I guess this hour is wasted! I might as well go home!"
Competent _____ Incompetent _____

"No book today, huh? How do you want to handle this?"
Competent _____ Incompetent _____

Besides leaving responsibility for the problem with the speaker, active listening also involves suspending judgment while the speaker decides how to handle the problem.

Speaker: I think I'm going to drop this class.

Advice: Oh, don't do that! You need this class to get your degree! It would be a terrible mistake to drop it now!

Commiseration: I know how you feel. It's a hard course with lots of homework. I wouldn't blame you for dropping it.

Blame: After all the time I have spent helping you with this class, how can you even *think* of dropping it!

Active Listening: Thinking about hanging it up, huh?

Notice that the active listening response is the only one that invites the speaker to continue talking without needing to defend her statement. All the other responses assume that the speaker has made up her mind, that she plans to proceed in a certain way, and that she needs or wants advice. The active listening response suspends judgment. This allows the person to continue talking as she sorts out her thoughts without needing to decide at this moment whether she really means everything she is saying. She has the freedom to remain uncommitted until she decides for sure whether she wants to drop the class or stay in it.

Let's look at the conversation again.

Speaker: I think I'm going to drop this class.

Active Listener: Thinking about hanging it up, huh?

Speaker: Yes. You've been a great help, and I really enjoy the class, but my Dad's real sick and I need to spend time with him rather than in school.

Active Listener: Seems like you don't have time for both, huh?

Speaker: No, I don't. Not unless I cut back my work hours. Come to think of it, that's probably a better idea! I'll see if I can work less hours and still keep my job. That way I could spend more time with Dad and still graduate on time. I'll check on that today.

Notice that the speaker came to her own conclusion. The active listener did not express an opinion or give advice. By suspending judgment the active listener allowed the speaker to explore her ideas without being held responsible for them. This is a loving act, to suspend judgment until the other person is sure about what she wants to say and feels finished. It is not easy. Yet for the speaker it can be a powerful experience. It feels like being understood. It feels like being listened to in a way that counts.

The speaker is not the only person who benefits from active listening. It can also be a powerful experience for the listener. When we listen so that we really hear another person we may receive some surprises. The people in our lives may be saying different things than we expected. We may not like all that we hear. We may find that it is necessary for us to develop a whole new level of tolerance to cope with some of these experiences. As Robin Norwood suggests in *Women Who Love Too Much* (Simon & Schuster, 1986), we may find that we must stop managing and controlling the people in our lives—for their good and for our own. On the other hand, we may hear a lot more love than we ever imagined. The only requirement is that we listen long enough to hear it.

Active Listening Practice

Respond to the following statements in a way that uses the active listening skills covered in this lesson.

1. Student: I missed class for two weeks because my kids were sick and now I am really behind. There's a test tomorrow!

   Tutor: _____

   _____

2. Student: I don't have much time to spend on my homework and reading. If you help me with those I should be able to pass the class.

   Tutor: _____

   _____

3. Student: Sorry I missed our session last week. My car is not dependable.

   Tutor: _____

   _____

4. Student: Mr. Pound never gives us any help. If you ask questions in class he just tells you that you should have been listening.

   Tutor: _____

   _____

Practice with People in Your Life

Try active listening with people in your life: tutees, friends, family. Choose one dialog to share and write it up in about one page.

Notice the Difference!

Write at least 50 words describing how active listening has made a difference in your relationships.

U N I T 3

READING AND STUDY SKILLS

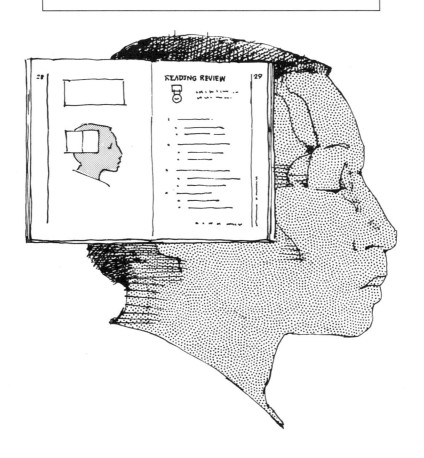

LESSON 7: REDUCING TEXT ANXIETY

OBJECTIVES

In this lesson you will have the opportunity to:
1. Help tutees reduce test anxiety by putting tests into a realistic perspective.
2. Help tutees learn how to get better grades on tests.

This lesson looks at five ways to reduce test anxiety:
1. Understand the reasons for tests.
2. Understand the limits of tests.
3. Feel better about ourselves as test takers.
4. Use test-taking skills.
5. Prepare for the test.

PRACTICE

Complete the exercises in this lesson with a tutee. If you are not currently tutoring, any other student may work with you.

How to Reduce Test Anxiety

Understanding the Reasons for Tests

With your student, think about the reasons why college students must take tests. List at least 10 reasons for taking tests:

1. _____   6. _____
2. _____   7. _____
3. _____   8. _____
4. _____   9. _____
5. _____   10. _____

Now read over your list. Some of your reasons were more serious than others. Put an asterisk by the one or two reasons that seem most important to you. If possible compare lists with another student. Notice how the lists are similar and how they are different. Ask an instructor to name several reasons why college students must take tests. Notice differences and similarities between the instructor's and the students' answers. Then complete the following exercise.

The Reasons for Tests

Insights I gained about reasons why college students are tested:

_____

_____

Understanding the Limits of Tests

Think about the meanings of test scores. Complete the following exercise.

The Limits of Tests

What a test can tell about me _____

_____

What a test can never tell about me _____

_____

What I can learn about myself from my test results _____

_____

What my instructor can learn from my test results _____

_____

Feeling Better about Ourselves as Test Takers

Complete the following exercise.

Feelings about Tests

Some reasons why tests scare me:

_____

_____

_____

_____

When I feel good about myself I do better on tests because:

_____

_____

_____

_____

How does one stop being scared and start feeling good about taking tests? There are two ways to do this. One is to replace the negative messages in our heads—the messages that make us expect to fail—with positive messages. The other way is to prepare ourselves thoroughly for a test.

We all have negative messages in our heads which remind us of our past mistakes and current shortcomings, usually at the times when we feel most vulnerable. If we allow ourselves to listen to these negative messages, we become fearful and stupid. We behave as if the negative messages are the only truth about us!

On the other hand, it is possible simply to acknowledge the negative messages when they occur, then to let go of them and replace them with positive messages about ourselves. Positive messages remind us of our best qualities and encourage us to behave as if our best qualities were the only truth about us! For example, I know that at least sometimes I am a capable, competent, mature adult. The more I remind myself about the capable, competent, mature aspect of my character, the more I behave as if I were completely capable, competent, and mature. When I remind myself of these good qualities before and during a test, I am likely to perform as a capable, competent, mature person.

Complete the following exercise.

Negative and Positive Messages

Some negative messages that I hear in my head before a test:

_____

_____

_____

Some positive messages that I need to hear before a test (examples: I think clearly; I easily remember everything I need to know):

_____

_____

_____

I remind myself that *I am a capable, competent, mature adult.* (Write out the words in italics.)

_____

Complete the following sentences:

I am capable when I _____

_____

I am competent when I _____

_____

I am a mature adult when I _____

_____

I am a Capable, Competent, Mature Adult. Say this to yourself 100 times a day for five days before any test. Say it to yourself immediately before the test, and at least five times during the test. Do the same with the other positive messages that you need to hear. You may be surprised at the results!

Use Test-Taking Skills

These techniques can help you focus on a test with the clear intention of receiving the highest score possible:

1. Follow directions
2. Look over the test
3. Plan your strategy
4. Do the easy ones first
5. Check your work.

Follow Directions. Listen carefully to the spoken instructions. Ask any questions about the test before it begins.

Read written directions carefully so that you answer the question. Many students lose points because they begin writing answers without understanding the question. For example, if the question reads "define pasteurization," and instead I write an essay about the *benefits* of pasteurization, I will forfeit all the points for that question. It will not matter if I knew the answer or not. Read the directions carefully, ask questions if you do not understand what is expected, then answer the exact question asked.

Look Over the Test. Before you begin, write down any formulas that you will need. Next, take a look at the whole test. This gives you a sense of direction and allows your subconscious mind to begin working on parts of the test that may initially puzzle you.

Plan Your Strategy. Remember that unless the directions state otherwise, you may answer questions in any order you wish. Choose the order that assists you. Do the easy ones first. Make a mark beside questions that you skip, so it will be easy to find them the second time around.

If the test is timed, decide how much time you will spend on each section. If the test involves an essay, jot down a quick outline of the points you will cover.

Do the Easy Ones First. Many students lose points by laboring over one difficult problem until the time is up and leave blank some easier problems that could have added points to their scores.

For example, let us imagine that a math test has 10 problems, each worth 10 points. The total possible score is 100 points. If the test is timed for one hour, a student may decide to spend no more than 5 minutes on each problem, leaving 10 minutes to check his work before handing in the test. This is a good test strategy. However, let's suppose that the fourth problem takes more than 5 minutes. In fact the student spends 20 minutes on the problem and still feels uncertain about the result. Reluctantly he goes on to the fifth problem, which takes him 10 minutes.

Forty-five minutes have now passed. If the remaining problems each take 5 minutes the student will complete only 8 problems and have no time to check his work. Problems 6 and 7 take 5 minutes each. Problem 8 takes 4 minutes, but the one remaining minute is not enough for the student to finish another problem. Assume that the student received all the possible points for seven problems and no points for the fourth problem. His total score will be 70%; that is, a D.

Now let's suppose that the student took the test doing the easy ones first. He does the first three problems, skips problem 4 skips problem 5, and completes the remaining problems in 4 minutes each. He now has almost 15 minutes to finish the test. He looks again at problem 4 and decides to try problem 5 first. He spends 10 minutes on problem 5. In the remaining time he checks problem 4 again, decides to skip it again, and uses the remaining time to check his work. Assuming that he receives all the possible points for each problem he completed, his score will be 90%; that is, an A −. This student still did not know how to do problem four, but the penalty was much less because he did the easy ones first. He received points for all the problems that he was able to do.

Check Your Work. Plan to leave some time at the end of the test period to check your work for errors. Spelling, punctuation, and small math mistakes are some examples of corrections that could add significantly to your score.

Be Prepared for the Test

Preparation for a test begins on the first day of class. It includes:

1. Regular study
2. Timely homework
3. Review
4. Rest

Regular Study means taking notes in class and rewriting them after class. It means getting together with other students in the class to compare class notes. This allows you to fill in any parts that you missed and clear up any misunderstandings. Regular study also means reading the text and highlighting or taking notes on the most important parts.

Regular study includes explaining the text to at least one other person, as a check on our own understanding. (We are not able to explain something unless we understand it.) If we explain parts of the text to another student in the class, and that person also explains parts of the lesson to us, we may find that it is not necessary for each person to read all of the text. In fact some students form study groups that assign chapters to members. Each member studies his or her chapter thoroughly and explains it to everyone else.

The important thing to remember is that regular study involves more than going to class and reading the text. Regular study means knowing the material.

Timely Homework means keeping up with homework assignments and turning them in on time. This prevents falling behind in the class. It allows problems to surface early so that they can be resolved before tests begin.

Review means going back over your notes on a regular basis—such as once a week—rather than waiting until the night before a test. Review keeps the information fresh so that you do not forget what you have learned. Review makes it possible to keep calm on the night before a test, because you know that you are prepared.

Rest means getting enough sleep, especially on the night before a test, so that you are ready to do your best.

LESSON 8: EFFICIENT READING

OBJECTIVE

In this lesson you will have the opportunity to learn and practice ten strategies for efficient college reading, which you will then pass on to your tutees.

PRACTICE

Guide a student through the Ten Strategies for Efficient Reading, using the Practice Questions at the end of the lesson.

How to Teach Efficient Reading

Most college students would like to read more, in less time, and with increased understanding. Often students who seek a tutor really need a reading coach. Many tutors are themselves efficient readers, but they may not know how to explain reading techniques to other students. This lesson presents ten strategies that a tutor can use to help another person read efficiently.

Evan, who had always been a good reader, was surprised to learn that reading requires new techniques in college. Gone forever are the days when he could read the chapter through once and be ready for a test. Many college students find themselves in serious academic trouble before they realize this.

In college reading you are expected not only to understand the material, but also to recall it, evaluate it, and compare it with other material on the same subject.

College reading is challenging. Most students find that they are expected to do more reading than ever before, and that most of the reading is difficult. There are ten strategies that can make college reading more efficient:

1. Describe the purpose for reading
2. Make sure you have the necessary background
3. Highlight the main points
4. React to the message
5. Learn the new vocabulary
6. Write exam questions
7. Estimate the time needed for study
8. Compare this information with other information
9. Apply this information to the world you know
10. Review

Teaching Efficient Reading (Continued)

The rest of this lesson will explain how to use these ten strategies for efficient reading.

1. | Describe the Purpose for Reading

Before you begin a reading assignment, have a clear understanding of your purpose for reading the material. Ask yourself what you want to be able to do after you read this selection. Do you want to pass a test, to lead a discussion, to write a paper? For each of these purposes you should read the material in a different way.

To prepare for a test, try to guess what the questions will be by turning headings and new vocabulary into questions. For example, to study this lesson on efficient reading, you would turn the heading Efficient Reading into a question: What is efficient reading? The answer includes the ten strategies for efficient reading. Each of the ten strategies then becomes a question. The first strategy, describe the purpose for reading, becomes the question: How do I describe the purpose for reading? As you construct and answer these questions, you tailor your reading to prepare for the test.

To prepare to lead a discussion, you would read with a different purpose. Instead of making up questions, you would identify controversial issues in the material. You would look for information that could support each side of the controversy. With this information you would create questions to probe those issues in a discussion.

To write a paper, focus your attention on only one aspect of the reading assignment. Then supplement that information with other readings on the same subject. For example, to write a paper about Intentions as they are described in this book, you would read Lesson 1, then read other sources to get additional information on the subject.

The purpose guides the reading, allowing you to get what you need from the material without wasting time.

2. | Make Sure You Have the Necessary Background

No one can learn something totally new just by reading about it. Efficient reading requires some previous experience with the topic. For example, most people would find it difficult or impossible to assemble a computer with only an instruction booklet and a box of parts. We could certainly read the words in the booklet, but without knowing something about how computers are put together, most of us would be unable to complete the task alone. The persons who could complete the task alone are those who have some background related to computer assembly.

The same principle applies to reading instructions on how to play a musical instrument, or knit an afghan. One needs experience with these activities before one can read with understanding. In the same way, a student needs to have the necessary background to read a textbook with understanding. No amount of reading and rereading will make sense of the material unless a student knows something about it in the first place.

How do you know if you have enough background? Examine the textbook by first reading the introductory chapter. Does it make sense to you? Look at the pictures, look at the table of contents, look through the various chapters. Is there anything here that you recognize? For example, in a microbiology textbook you might read about cells, plasma, and microscopes in the introductory chapter. If you have no idea what these things are or how they function, you should consider yourself in need of more background information. Without the background you need, you are at serious risk of getting a low grade in the course. The more background you have when you begin the course, the more likely that you will get the top grade you want.

How to get instant background. It is possible to gain background by taking an introductory course to prepare yourself. A quick alternative is to give yourself an overview of the subject by using an encyclopedia, videos, and knowledgeable people to fill you in.

The *World Book Encyclopedia* provides basic information on almost any subject, without confusing terminology and without unnecessary details.

A video or a movie may provide excellent background, but you may need to watch it more than once to absorb everything.

A knowledgeable person can also provide the background you need, if you can locate such a person. The instructor or a friend may be able to help you find a person who would enjoy sharing his or her knowledge with you. It is quite possible that you will have some knowledge to share in return.

3. Highlight the Main Points

As you read each section, underline or highlight the main point with a colored marker designed for this purpose. This takes at least two readings, so do not try to rush. If you do not read the section through first, you may highlight way too much. If you highlight too much there is no benefit to highlighting at all! So read carefully, select only the most important parts, and highlight those.

Teaching Efficient Reading (Continued)

Confused about what is important? Use this quick test:

- Is it mentioned in the heading?
- Was it mentioned in the lecture?
- Is it repeated in the book?
- Is it part of a series (For example, one of the seven basic food groups)?
- Is it set off by special print (italics or boldface type)?

If the answer is "Yes" to one or more of these questions, the information is important and should be highlighted.

4. React to the Message

Read as if you are having a conversation with the author. Question, argue, cheer, disagree—but react. Your reactions involve you in the material in a way that helps you remember it. For example, you might ask questions something like these as you read: What does this mean? Who is that? What does the author mean here? Can this be true?

Write your questions and comments in the margins or in a notebook. Keep a special list of questions to ask your instructor during class.

5. Learn the New Vocabulary

It is absolutely essential to use correctly the vocabulary of the subject you are studying. You can learn the vocabulary in the lectures, labs, study groups, and from the readings.

Jot down a definition whenever you hear a new term, and write or draw an example to remind yourself how to use the word correctly.

Make flash cards—3" × 5" cards that have the new word on one side and the meaning on the other side. Use the flash cards to practice the vocabulary until you know it. Carry your flash cards with you so that you can use time for studying that might otherwise be wasted waiting for buses, etc.

Whenever you are uncertain how to pronounce a word, check the glossary in your textbook. If you still have a question, bring it up in class or in your study group.

6. Write Exam Questions

One of the most effective techniques for remembering what you have read is to write your own exam questions. As you finish reading each section, create an exam question that could test a student's understanding of that section. Then create another question to test understanding of how the section fits into the chapter or the book.

Your exam questions might begin with words like these:

- Define . . .
- Explain who/what/where/when/why/how . . .
- Compare and contrast . . .

The exam you actually take may not include an essay. But writing this type of question will help you focus your attention on the key concepts and their relationships to each other. Each time you think of the question and the answer, you will set the information more firmly in your memory.

7. Estimate the Time Needed for Study

It takes time to absorb new information. When we try to rush the learning process we often forget more than we remember. It is important to take the time that is necessary to assure our success.

College costs a great deal of money. You might consider the expense to be an investment in your future. One way to protect that investment is to take the time you need to learn and know thoroughly the material that you are studying.

- Take the time to reread.
- Take the time to make notes.
- Take the time to create exam questions.
- Take the time to review.
- Take the time to remember what you need to know.

Remember, for most students this amounts to at least two hours outside of class for every hour of class time.

Teaching Efficient Reading (Continued)

8. | Compare This Information with Other Information

One of the joys of being a student is the opportunity to explore diverse opinions. The information in your textbook is only a sample of the information available on that subject. Chances are good that you had some knowledge of the subject before you started the class. As you read and study the material for the course, compare the information that you are learning with your previous knowledge and with other information that you gain from lectures, discussions, etc.

Some of the information in your textbook may conflict with information that you collect from other sources. When this happens, compare the differing opinions by asking yourself some questions about them. Your questions might be something like these:

• What are the areas of consistency with what I know?

• What are the areas of inconsistency with what I know?

• Does this selection contain information that is new to me?

• If so, what are the sources of this new information?

• How reliable is it?

• Is it possible that this information is incorrect?

• Is it possible that my previous information is not complete?

• Is it possible for me to develop a new way of looking at this information?

It is often helpful to make a chart to compare points of view. Your chart might look something like this:

Opinion A	Opinion B
The world is round.	The world is square.
Physics and observations tell us that the world is round.	The Bible refers to the four corners of the earth.
Photos from space show that the world is round.	Photos from space are a hoax.

9. | Apply This Information to the World You Know |

As you finish reading each section or chapter, take a few minutes to think about what you have read. Try to summarize the material in your head. Then try to form an opinion or come to a conclusion about what you have read. Try to see how the information could apply to a familiar situation in your life. Consider problems that might occur, and also try to imagine new possibilities.

For example, after reading about the elements of a healthy diet, you might first try to recall what those elements are. You might then form an opinion, such as: "A healthy diet would be good for me." Next, you might consider applying the new information to your diet. For example, you might decide that your diet should include more whole grains and vegetables and less fat.

Applying the information to the world you know also involves a check on reality. Perhaps you should eat more whole grains and vegetables and consume less fat—but are you really willing to do this? There may be factors pulling you in both directions. Perhaps you want to be healthy and slim, but the foods you like are refined, processed, and full of fat.

Applying the information to the world you know means considering problems and looking for new possibilities. Perhaps you could imagine a way to eat foods you like while also improving your diet. For example, you might be willing to eat the foods you like in smaller quantities, along with eating some healthier foods. Or you might learn to prepare the foods that you like in healthier ways.

10. | Review |

Without review, everyone forgets about 33 percent of what they have learned within a day and almost everything they have learned within a week. After reading, keep the information current in your mind by regularly reviewing the highlighted parts of the book, along with your questions and comments. Whenever possible, discuss the material with other students. Use it, go over it, think about it, talk about it. Every review fixes the information more firmly in your memory.

Practice Questions

Ask a tutee (or a friend) the following questions. Write down his or her answers.

1. What are you reading (the title)? _____

_____

_____

2. Why are you reading it? (Describe the purpose for reading.) _____

_____

_____

3. Summarize the main points in the selection. _____

_____

_____

4. Give your reaction to the passage. _____

_____

_____

5. Define three new or uncommon vocabulary words in the selection. ____

_____

_____

6. Write three exam questions about the material. _____

_____

_____

7. Estimate the time needed to study and learn this information. _____

_____

_____

8. Compare the information in this selection with other information from your
background. _____

_____

_____

9. Choose a way to apply this information to the world you know. _____

_____

_____

10. Explain how often you will review this information and why. _____

_____

_____

LESSON 9: WRITING OUTSTANDING PAPERS

OBJECTIVE

> In this lesson you will have the opportunity to learn how to assist other students to write outstanding college papers.

PRACTICE

> Guide a student through the A+ Formula using the Practice section at the end of the lesson.

How to use the A+ Formula

The A+ Formula is a guide for students who want to write great papers in the shortest possible time. This lesson explains the three parts of an A+ paper:

1. *The opening* introduces the topic, the point of view, and the structure of the paper.
2. *The development* expands the topic and provides evidence to support the opening statement.
3. *The completion* provides a recap of the points made in the paper, along with a fresh insight.

It may be encouraging to know that few "A" papers are written by gifted writers. Most are written by ordinary students who share the secrets of good writing. The A+ Formula will help you to write effective papers in subjects as diverse as microbiology, English, and political science.

The A+ Formula (Continued)

THE OPENING

An outstanding paper begins with a statement that introduces the topic, the point of view, and the structure of the paper that follows. In the A+ Formula the opening features *a paradox*—a statement that appears to be a contradiction, but contains a kernel of truth. Typical paradoxes involve such contrasts as light/dark, good/evil, weak/strong, end/beginning, wise/foolish. The following are examples of some paradoxes written by college students.

Speed may be fun, but it is not funny.

Cigarettes bring comfort and relaxation to the smoker as they quietly ravage her health.

Carbon is the element of life, death, and regeneration.

San Francisco, the fourth largest metropolitan area in the United States, provides many of the comforts of a small town for the residents of its ethnic neighborhoods.

Research into child abuse has shown that the abusers were themselves victims of child abuse.

Too few vitamins can make you sick; too many can kill you.

A paradox is a strong opening because it's surprising. It challenges the reader to find the explanation by reading on. Constructing a paradox challenges the writer to expand his or her current way of looking at the world.

How to Write a Paradox. First, select the general topic of the paper, and write it down.

On a piece of scratch paper, write down as many contradictions in the topic as you can think of. This step should take 10-15 minutes.

Choose some of the contradictions that appeal to you. Mark your choices with an X.

Try out some of the contradictions in sample sentences. Write for 10-15 minutes.

Choose two of the sample sentences and refine them for possible opening statements.

Select the one opening statement that best states your point of view. Refine it further if necessary.

The A+ Formula (Continued)

Example

1. Topic of paper: Ethnic culture in San Francisco

2. Brainstorm possible contradictions.
   separate/together   old/new   good/bad   city/town
   diversity/sameness   large/small

3. Choose some that appeal to you.

4. Try out some sample sentences.

   City/town: San Francisco seems like a small town when you are in an ethnic neighborhood.

   Separate/together: Ethnic neighborhoods provide foreign immigrants with a sense of belonging.

   Large/small: San Francisco, the fourth largest metropolitan area in the United States, has ethnic neighborhoods that feel like villages.

5. Refine two or more as possible opening statements.

   The San Francisco Metropolitan area, fourth largest in the United States, is a panoply of ethnic neighborhoods which provide many of the comforts of a village or a small town to the disparate residents.

   San Francisco, the fourth largest metropolitan area in the United States, provides many of the comforts of a small town for the residents of its ethnic neighborhoods.

THE DEVELOPMENT

The paper develops through the presentation of evidence that supports the opening statement. This is the longest part of the paper. In a five page paper the development comprises about four pages.

A paradox in the opening statement leads naturally into a comparison/contrast structure for the development of the topic. A comparison/contrast paper usually develops by first comparing the likenesses, then contrasting the differences, of each aspect of the opening statement. For example, the opening paradox about San Francisco could be developed beginning like this:

> Neighborhoods are places where the faces in the crowded city have names, families, and sorrows. Respect, honor, courage, and love occur here at least as often as contempt, fear, and hate. The neighborhood grocery, the local bar, the playground, the laundry, the bus stop, the church: these are the meeting places of the community. Conversations whispered here affect the residents as much as the loftiest proclamations signed in City Hall.

Information supporting the opening statement may be taken from published sources, recorded observations, interviews, or personal experiences. Published sources may be books or periodicals, as well as encyclopedias and other standard reference materials. Recorded observations are the result of carefully watching what is going on and making notes about it. Observations often take place in a lab; but they can take place anywhere. Interviews are structured discussions in which the writer asks prepared questions of a knowledgeable person, and records the person's exact responses. Personal experiences may be used as supporting information. In a college paper, they are usually secondary to documented evidence.

We all understand new material better when it relates to something we have experienced. Supporting information should therefore be presented in a way that relates to the reader's experience. You can connect your paper to the reader's experience with anecdotes, analogies, examples, and visual aids.

An anecdote is a brief story from real life which is used to illustrate a point. For example, a paper about neighborhoods in San Francisco might include an anecdote about the 80-year-old flower lady of the Mission District. Anecdotes may come from your experience or your observations. In order to avoid possible embarrassment to the people involved, never use real names in anecdotes. Change the age and sex of the people if you wish. You may occasionally choose to disguise your own experiences as those of an anonymous ''Barbara'' or ''Sam.''

An *analogy* is the comparison of an unfamiliar thing with something more familiar or easier to understand.

For example, the parts of the human eye are often explained using the analogy of a camera. War has often been compared to a game of chess. Knowledge has been compared to a light shining in the darkness. An analogy is a good technique for clarifying a complicated idea.

An *example* is the selection of one item from a group to show what the whole group is like. Sugar is an example of a carbohydrate; gasoline is an example of a nonrenewable resource; ¾ is an example of a fraction. Examples keep the readers involved by connecting the subject of the paper with something familiar to them.

Visual aids are pictures or diagrams that show the reader what you are talking about. If the paper is about a person, include a photograph; if the paper is about a country, include a map; if the paper is about the operation of an engine, include a diagram. Visual aids make the subject clear in a way that is not possible with words alone.

THE COMPLETION

The A+ paper finishes with a brief summary of the points made, followed by a generalization and a synthesis.

The generalization is an opinion or a conclusion which logically follows from the information the paper has presented. It is often immediately followed by a synthesis. A sample generalization:

> Far from being lost in the anonymity of a big city, folks in the Sunset neighborhood of San Francisco they know that they belong.

The synthesis closes the paper with a fresh insight dramatizes the essential message of the work. The generalization quoted above might be followed by this synthesis:

> ''Weird Harold'' shoots spitballs at them!

The A+ Formula works for research papers as well as for essays. However, the research paper has special requirements, such as a bibliography of sources consulted and footnotes crediting authors for paraphrases or quoted material. Students writing research papers are urged to use one of the excellent guidebooks on the market, such as Kate Turabian's *A Manual for Writers of Term Papers, Theses, and Dissertations*. The A+ Formula can be used for the overall structure of the paper.

Finishing Touches

Your final copy should be neatly typed, with accurate spelling, correct grammar, and proper punctuation. If you have difficulty in any of these areas, get help right away. Your college's learning resource center, or study skills center, is there to help you (see Lesson 11). You may find a course, a lab, a video tape, or a computer program that is just what you need. Go there today!

Practice

Use this guide to help a tutee (or a friend) practice the three parts of the A+ Formula:

1. Write a paradox to open a paper for a subject that you are studying this term.
2. Give evidence to support your opening statement. Identify the source(s) of the evidence.

   Create an anecdote, an analogy, an example, or a visual aid to connect your paper to the reader's experience.
3. Write a completion to the paper above: a generalization and a synthesis.

LESSON 10: IMPROVING MEMORY

OBJECTIVES

In this lesson you will have the opportunity to improve your memory by developing:
1. **Effective study habits.**
2. **Efficient note-taking skills.**
3. **Productive study groups.**

PRACTICE

1. **Complete the Study Habits worksheet.**
2. **Take class notes using the format illustrated in Figure 1.**
3. **Complete the Study Group report.**

How to Improve Memory

College students are deluged with information to remember. At times it may seem too much—the memory may be overloaded and tempted to shut down. At such times many students seek out a tutor. What can a tutor do to assist a student who wants a better memory? This lesson will cover effective study habits, efficient note-taking skills, and productive study groups.

Effective Study Habits

Many students enroll in college classes without realizing the amount of study time that is expected. On the average, students should expect to spend 2-3 hours outside of class for every hour spent in class. This means for every 3-unit class a student should expect to spend 6-9 hours per week studying outside of class. Students with learning disabilities and those whose knowledge of English is limited should expect to study longer. Students who work or have families should consider the time element when deciding how many courses to take.

A study schedule helps many students plan their time efficiently. Most students learn best if they study several subjects for short periods each day rather than studying one subject for several hours. For example, Jean studies French from 1:00 to 2:00, physics from 2:00 to 3:00, and history from 3:00 to 4:00 each day. Marilyn also studies from 1:00 to 4:00 each day; on Mondays she studies French for 3 hours, on Tuesdays physics, and on Wednesdays history. Jean's approach keeps the information fresh and aids memory.

During study time it is important to have a quiet, well-lighted place, free from distractions. The library is often a good place to study.

Efficient Note-taking Skills

Reading notes were discussed in Lesson 8. Lecture notes are discussed here.

Efficient note taking begins with effective listening. Effective listening in the classroom is just as important as reading the textbook. Many instructors present material in class that is not covered in the book. Also, most instructors emphasize in class the important concepts that will appear on tests.

Effective listening begins before the class begins. The effective listener has the necessary books and materials before the first class. Effective listeners read outside assignments and complete homework before each class. They often come to class with reading notes, which they expand during the lecture. One way to do this is to fold notepaper in half the long way, writing notes from your reading on the left-hand side and related notes from the lecture on the right. (Reading notes for the present chapter are shown in Figure 1.) Topics that are covered in both the lecture and the reading are likely to appear on a test.

Efficient note takers are prepared to hear and write down the main ideas of a lecture. They recognize the main ideas (1) because they have been covered in the reading, or (2) because they are emphasized by the instructor. Main ideas are usually signaled by words like these:

basic concept	major development
theory	movement
trend	major work
important idea	era
principle	

These signal words are often followed by numerical words such as:

four causes
first . . . . second . . . third . . .
three major effects
two reasons

Examples may be given in the various numerical categories and these should be written down and labeled as examples. Leave space to write in other examples of your own as you study the notes later. A summary or conclusion may be signaled by words such as:

therefore	so
consequently	in conclusion
accordingly	thus

Write down as much of the summary or conclusion as possible, since this provides a check on whether you have gotten the main points of the lecture.

Even the best notetakers occasionally have moments when they miss explanations or misunderstand concepts. Their notes may be incomplete or confusing. An effective way to complete the lecture is to meet immediately after class with a group of other students to compare notes and fill in missing parts. The next section explains how study groups can improve your memory.

Productive Study Groups

A study group can improve your memory because the group will always remember more than one person can. Most study groups meet immediately after class or later the same day to complete notes, ask questions, and discuss the lecture. Assignments and homework are also discussed and sometimes worked on together. Group members explain difficult concepts to each other until everyone understands. The person who does the explaining often benefits even more than the person who receives the information. Some people suggest having at least one poor student in every study group so that group members can benefit by explaining everything to that person.

The secret to improving memory is to become actively involved in the learning process. Effective study habits, efficient note-taking skills, and productive study groups are the means to active involvement. Expanded memory is the natural result.

Study Habits Worksheet

1. I am taking _____ units. I plan to study _____ hours per week.

   _____ (units) × 2 (or 3) hours = _____ hours per week.

2. My study schedule is complete (Yes _____ No _____). If not complete, it will

   be ready by _____

Class Notes

Use the format described in this chapter and illustrated in Figure 1 to take notes in one class—and to keep taking them in all your classes.

Study Group Report

Are you part of a study group?   Yes _____   No _____

Describe your study group (or explain why you're not in one).

_____

_____

_____

_____

_____

_____

_____

_____

_____

_____

_____

Reading Notes

1. Effective study habits
   a. study schedule
      1) 2-3 hrs. per wk. per unit
      2) short time per subj. per day
   b. quiet! (library)

2. Efficient note-taking skills
   a. effective listening
   b. main points
   c. examples
   d. summary/conclusion

3. Productive study groups
   a. complete notes
   b. ask questions
   c. discuss lecture

Lecture Notes

Figure 1.   Reading notes for Lesson 10

LESSON 11: USING LEARNING RESOURCES

OBJECTIVES

In this lesson you will have the opportunity to:
1. Get acquainted with the learning center.
2. Get acquainted with the college library.
3. Find out where and how to locate the information you need.
4. Find out where and how to assist a tutee in locating information.

PRACTICE

1. Complete the learning center questionnaire.
2. Complete the library questionnaire.
3. Answer the Review Questions at the end of the lesson.

How to Make Learning Resources Work for You

Finding the answers to the questions listed below will help you find your way around the learning center and the library.

Learning Center Questionnaire

A learning center may also be called the learning resource center, the learning skills center, the student learning center, or the communication skills lab. Write the name for your college's learning center here: _____

Go to the learning center at your college and find out the answers to the following questions.

1. The learning center hours are _____

2. Does your learning center offer classes? Yes _____ No _____
   If so, list them below

   _____   _____

   _____   _____

   _____   _____

   _____   _____

3. Is the tutoring program located in the learning center? Yes _____ No _____

   a. How does one become a tutor? _____

     _____

   b. How does one arrange to receive help from a tutor? _____

4. Is there a writing lab in the learning center? Yes _____ No _____

   a. If yes, what are the hours? _____

   b. If no, is it located somewhere else on campus? _____

     _____

   c. Who may use the writing lab? _____

     _____

   d. Why would a student use the writing lab? _____

     _____

5. Is there a math lab in the learning center? Yes _____ No _____

   a. If yes, what are the hours? _____

   b. If no, is it located somewhere else on campus? _____

     _____

   c. Who may use the math lab? _____

     _____

   d. Why would a student use the math lab? _____

     _____

6. Is there a foreign language lab in the learning center? Yes _____ No _____

7. Are placement tests given in the learning center? Yes _____ No _____

   a. If no, where are placement tests given? _____

     _____

   b. Who should take placement tests? _____

     _____

   c. Why take a placement test? _____

     _____

8. What are the other functions of the learning center?

   _____

   _____

   _____

9. How do you, or could you, use the learning center?

_____

_____

_____

_____

10. How do you, or could you, use the learning center with your tutees?

_____

_____

_____

_____

Library Questionnaire

Go to the library and find out the answers to the following questions.

1. The library hours are _____

2. What classification system is used at the library? _____

_____

3. What periodicals are available in the subjects(s) you are tutoring?

_____   _____

_____   _____

_____   _____

_____   _____

4. What is a microfiche? _____

_____

5. What services and facilities are available at your library?

_____

_____

_____

_____

6. What is the name of one reference librarian? _____

   a. How could a reference librarian help you? _____

   _____

   b. How could a reference librarian help a tutee? _____

   _____

Review Questions

What discoveries did you make at the learning center?

_____

_____

_____

_____

What discoveries did you make at the library?

_____

_____

_____

_____

How will the information in this lesson help you to be a better tutor?

_____

_____

_____

_____

UNIT 4

STUDENTS WITH SPECIAL NEEDS AND STUDENTS AT RISK

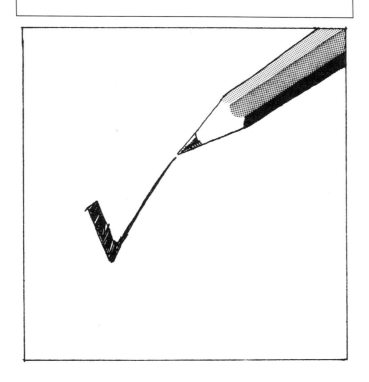

I have been asked to tutor student athletes. What special information do I need?

Student athletes present special challenges to a tutor for these reasons:

1. Demanding schedules of practice and games may leave student athletes little time for study.

2. Student athletes may frequently miss classes for travel.

3. Athletes may not be interested in academics. They may be attending college primarily to play sports.

4. Some athletes were passed through high school with minimal effort on their part. These athletes may expect the same treatment in college.

5. Some student athletes are recruited to attend colleges far away from home. There may be little support from family or friends to assist them in this transition.

The lessons in this book are designed to help you assist student athletes as well as other students with special needs.

LESSON 12: WHAT ARE SPECIAL NEEDS?

OBJECTIVES

In this lesson you will have the opportunity to:
1. Practice techniques for tutoring students who have special learning difficulties.
2. Identify the services available for disabled students at your college.

PRACTICE

Complete the Disabled Students Services exercise at the end of the lesson.

Who Are Students with Special Needs?

Students with special needs have learning difficulties. These may be due to specific learning disabilities, emotional problems, mental handicaps, or cultural differences.

A person with a learning disability has difficulty learning material in a specific area such as reading or math. The person functions normally in other areas.

A person with emotional problems has difficulty learning because of traumatic past experiences, which have left him or her feeling unworthy or stupid.

A person with a mental handicap has reduced functioning in many areas, usually due to a congenital defect, a serious injury, or an illness. With patience and good humor, these students can learn a great deal.

Students with cultural differences may have difficulty learning new material because they are coping with culture shock. This is discussed in Lesson 14.

All of these students need lots of encouragement through repeated positive messages. They also need clear explanations, repetition, and patience.

Techniques For Tutoring Special Students

These techniques apply regardless of the material that you are tutoring.

1. At the first meeting ask the student what he or she wants to accomplish through your sessions. Write down what the student says, because this is the goal for your tutoring relationship. When this goal is accomplished the tutoring relationship will end, unless another goal has been negotiated in the meantime.

2. Arrange a meeting with the student's instructor to find out what the student's particular needs are. Also arrange to talk to the college specialist in learning disabilities about special techniques that may help this student.

3. Spend the first 5 minutes of every session reviewing what you covered in the last meeting. Occasionally spend time reviewing major points covered so far.

4. Change activities frequently—at least every 15 or 20 minutes. Vary between using the book, using class notes, explaining, questioning, observing while the student works out sample problems, and listening to the student's concerns. Occasionally invite the student to get up and stretch or change position. Such a change of pace helps keep the student's attention focused on the material.

5. Select a location where the student faces a wall or a corner in order to avoid distractions.

6. Make constant eye contact with the student. This forces him or her to pay attention. When you break eye contact for quick moments look at the book— the student will tend to follow your glance.

7. Frequently invite the student to repeat back to you what he or she has just learned. This is the true test of how well he or she is comprehending. It also provides an extra practice (recitation).

8. When asking for a response from your student, wait at least 15 seconds for the reply. Avoid the urge to jump in and supply the answer just to break the silence. Your student needs to know that you really expect her or him to supply the information requested. In the past, she or he may have had responses discounted by others. She or he may not believe that you really expect her or him to know any answers. When you insist on a response, you demonstrate faith in the student's ability to comply. The student may resist at first, but her or his self-esteem will grow each time that she or he does respond.

9. Accept all responses respectfully. Try to find something right about any wrong answer, and use that to begin your gentle explanation of the correct information.

10. At the end of each session, review what has been covered and plan for the next meeting. Learning-disabled students are particularly in need of a structure, and schedule changes are upsetting. It is important to establish a routine and stick to it. Call in if you are unable to keep your tutoring appointment.

Disabled Student Services

Locate the disabled student services department at your college.

1. Find out the name and phone number of at least one contact person.

Name _____

Occupation _____

Telephone _____

2. Write down at least five services which are available for disabled students on your campus.

_____

_____

_____

_____

_____

_____

_____

_____

_____

_____

LESSON 13: WHAT IS IT LIKE TO BE DISABLED?

OBJECTIVES

In this lesson you will have the opportunity to:
1. Define various types of disabilities.
2. Experience for a few minutes what it is like to be disabled.
3. Discover ways that you can make a difference to a disabled person.
4. Discover ways that a disabled person can make a difference to you.

PRACTICE

1. Do the Practical Experience exercise to experience what life is like for a disabled person.
2. Complete the evaluation of your practical experience.
3. Do the Make a Difference exercise.

What Is It Like to Be Disabled?

There are two broad categories of disabilities: physical and mental. Examples of permanent physical disabilities are blindness, deafness, or the loss of an arm or leg. Examples of temporary physical disabilities are a broken arm, severe back pain, and other correctable physical problems.

Mental disabilites include mental retardation, in which functioning is impaired in many areas, and specific learning disabilities, such as dyslexia, in which functioning is impaired in only one area.

Practical Experience

With a partner, visit the college dining facility for a meal, a snack or a beverage. As you approach and leave the facility, and the entire time that you are inside, you must seriously impair your ability to function normally in *one* of these ways:

1. Wear someone else's glasses so that your vision is seriously impaired. Or, if you normally wear glasses, leave them off.
2. Wear earplugs (available at a pharmacy) so that you can hear little or nothing.
3. Stay in a wheelchair during the entire experience. You can borrow a wheelchair from Disabled Student Services if you explain that you need it for this course.

During the exercise DO attempt to socialize. DO NOT mention this course or the fact that you are doing an assignment.

The partner's job is to prevent injury, *not* to do things for you or to interfere with your experience.

Evaluation

1. How were you "disabled" in your Practical Experience? _____

2. Who was your partner? _____

3. How did people react to your disability?

   _____

   _____

   _____

   _____

4. What is it like to be "different"?

   _____

   _____

   _____

   _____

5. What practical problems did you have—opening doors, reading the menu, etc.?

   _____

   _____

   _____

   _____

   _____

6. Did anyone do anything that truly helped you?

   _____

   _____

   _____

   _____

7. List ten things that someone *could* have done truly to help you. (Assume that it is not possible to remove the disability or to practice magic.)

   _____   _____

   _____   _____

   _____   _____

   _____   _____

   _____   _____

8. List ten ways that you could make a difference to a disabled person.

_____ _____

_____ _____

_____ _____

_____ _____

_____ _____

Make a Difference

Arrange to spend at least 15 minutes with a disabled person. Do not mention this course or that you are doing an assignment. Then answer the following questions:

1. How did you make a difference to this person?

_____

_____

_____

_____

_____

_____

_____

_____

_____

2. How did this person make a difference to you?

_____

_____

_____

_____

_____

_____

_____

_____

_____

LESSON 14: COPING WITH CULTURAL DIFFERENCES

OBJECTIVES

In this lesson you will have the opportunity to:
1. Imagine what culture shock is like.
2. Identify some difficulties caused by cultural differences.
3. Explain some ways to overcome barriers caused by cultural differences.

PRACTICE

1. Use the Interviewer's Guide to interview a foreign student.
2. Complete the Interview Evaluation after the interview.

What Are Cultural Differences?

Culture is the sum of human civilization that we experience as normal and familiar. Culture includes the language, customs, religion, and history of a people.

We are not usually aware of our own culture until we travel to a foreign country where conditions are very different. Then the impact of a sudden, radical change in lifestyle and surroundings can produce culture shock. Culture shock occurs when conditions that we assumed were normal are suddenly out of place. For example, imagine yourself moving tomorrow to a country without paved roads, TV sets, refrigerators, or indoor plumbing.

How would it feel to be unfamiliar with the customs everyone else takes for granted? How would you fit into the social and gender roles expected of you? How would it feel for you, a college student, to be illiterate in the national language? How would you understand the lectures? How would you make friends?

Culture shock refers to the feelings of helplessness and inadequacy experienced by people who were well integrated in their native countries but now find themselves isolated in an unfamiliar society.

Foreigners who come to the United States often find the American lifestyle strange and disturbing. Those who attend college frequently find that their English is inadequate both for classes and for social purposes. They may speak with a heavy accent and have trouble understanding casual speech. As a result they often feel isolated and homesick.

Cultural Differences (Continued)

The American emphasis on punctuality and the pace of life in the United States may seem strange, even foolish. Some of our electronic technology may seem frightening. American foods may be unfamiliar and unappetizing. The social freedom that Americans enjoy may be threatening to some foreign students. To others, our social customs may seem rigid and silly.

Culture shock is disturbing, but it need not overwhelm your student. As the tutor, you may be able to help your student adjust to American life.

How Can I Help a Foreign Student?

With tolerance and humor you can build a bridge of understanding that both acknowledges and transcends culture. Get to know your student. You may be his or her first American friend. Take an interest in your student's cultural background. Encourage him or her to talk about family and friends at home. Explain American ways respectfully. Do not expect your student to want to become an instant American. Use common sense, relax, and enjoy your student as a person. You may make a greater difference in that person's life than you will ever know.

Interviewing a Foreign Student

In this activity you will meet a foreign student and interview him or her about differences in culture between his or her native country and the United States. Use the Interviewer's Guide in this lesson to assist you. The interview is intended to be informal. The interviewer should ask most of the questions, then write down the foreign student's responses. You may wish to tape-record the interview so that you do not have to write during the conversation.

How Will I Meet a Foreign Student?

You could approach a foreign student directly and express interest in the person's native country and background. Or you could ask an instructor, a classmate, or a mutual friend to introduce you. Most foreign students are eager to talk about their homelands and their adjustments to life in the United States.

Interviewer's Guide

Student's Name _____ Native Country _____
National language _____ Your native language _____
Your education in your native country _____
_____

Educational plans _____
_____

How long have you been in the United States? _____
How long do you plan to stay? _____
Why did you decide to come to the United States? _____
_____

Why did you decide to come to this college? _____
_____

Travels in the United States and elsewhere _____
_____

General impressions of life here _____
_____
_____

Did you speak English before you came here? _____
Did you read or write English? _____
If so, how did you learn it? _____

Has English been a problem for you? in classes? socially? other? Please explain.
_____

Have American customs been a problem for you ? Please explain. _____
_____
_____

What do you like about America? _____
_____

How would you change America if you could? _____
_____

What do you miss most about your country? _____
_____

How can other students help you to have a good experience here? _____
_____

Is there anything else that you could like to say? _____
_____
_____

Thank you for participating in this interview.

Interview Evaluation

Answer the following questions as you reflect on the interview.

What surprised me most about the interview was _____

_____

_____

_____

One important thing I learned from the interview was _____

_____

_____

_____

Cultural barriers that inhibited conversation during the interview _____

_____

_____

_____

How the student and I coped with these barriers _____

_____

_____

_____

Other comments

_____

_____

_____

_____

_____

_____

_____

_____

_____

_____

LESSON 15: STUDENTS AT RISK OF FAILING

OBJECTIVES

In this lesson you will have the opportunity to:
1. Identify whether your tutee is a student at risk of failing.
2. Learn what students at risk need.
3. Discover what a tutor can do to help.
4. Keep in mind what the tutor needs to do for himself or herself.

PRACTICE

1. Complete the Support exercise at the end of the lesson.
2. Do the Healing Opportunity exercise at the end of the lesson.

How to Assist Students at Risk of Failing

Students at risk of failing are difficult for tutors. No matter what the tutor does, these students often drop out or fail their classes. Students at risk of failing are often in difficult personal circumstances which reduce the time and energy available for study. Some of the characteristics of students at risk are:

1. On academic probation

2. Overloaded:
   - Too many work hours
   - Too many units
   - Too many activities
   - Too many responsibilities

3. Primary language other than English

4. Medical or emotional problems

5. Disruptive living conditions

6. Desperately low income

7. No career goals

8. Low self-esteem

9. Did not complete high school

10. Low grades in high school

11. Low economic expectations

If two or more of these circumstances describe your tutee, he or she should be considered a student at risk of failing.

What do these students need?

A Dream for the Future

Many students at risk have given little thought to what they want in the future. Often their lives so far have offered few choices. They may not expect to have many choices in the future either. Once these students realize that choices are available to them, they may be willing to think about what they want in the future.

Respect and Appreciation

Students at risk have often experienced failure and shame in high school. Now they need people in their lives who value them and believe in them. Mentors, friends, and peer groups are all possible sources of respect and appreciation.

A mentor is a special person who is interested in the student's dream, who believes that she can achieve it, and who will help her out along the way. A mentor may be a coach, a favorite teacher, a boss, a counselor, or an experienced friend. A mentor has already become successful in her field and she enjoys sharing her wisdom with a younger or less experienced person. A student at risk who finds a mentor will almost surely succeed in college.

As a tutor you may be the first to suggest the idea of a mentor to your student. You might also suggest possible mentors for the student.

No one can force another person to become their mentor, but there are ways of cultivating mentors. The following suggestions may help your student cultivate a mentor:

- Hang around the person as much as possible, but don't be a pest.
- Ask questions and listen to the answers.
- Let the person know that you respect her or him.
- Volunteer to help out with routine tasks.
- Tell others about your respect and admiration for the person.

Friends are important for everyone. However, students at risk may not have much time or energy for friends. You may be your student's first college friend. Treat him or her with respect and kindness while also encouraging him or her to make other friends. Introduce your tutees to each other and to other people you know.

A peer group may be a source of friends on campus. It may also give a student an important sense of belonging. Some peer groups that may appeal to your student include:

- Athletic teams

- Club memberships

- Classmates

- Students of similiar ethnic background

- Colleagues and co-workers

Structure

Your student may lack structure in his or her life. For example, she or he may lack some of the following:

- Time management skills (getting assignments in on time)

- Self-discipline (doing homework rather than watching TV)

- Stable living conditions (a safe, secure home)

- A reasonable schedule of classes, work, activities, and free time

It is often helpful to tell your student how you handle these situations in your life, rather than giving advice that may not be welcomed.

> If you are concerned about your student's health or safety please talk to your tutoring instructor or to a college counselor.

Success

Success may be an unfamiliar experience for your student. She or he needs success in college now. It is the responsibility of the student's college counselor to see to it that the student is enrolled in:

- Classes in which success is likely

- Remedial classes if needed

- Not too many classes

- Classes of interest to the student

Students sometimes do not get the help that they need from a college counselor. If your student seems to have a schedule that is too difficult for him or her to handle, you may want to talk to the counselor yourself. Explain the difficulties that you see.

What Can a Tutor Do to Help?

Healing opportunities are experiences that help your student to think of herself in a new, positive way. With your encouragement, she may come to believe she can do much more than she ever dared to imagine. Encourage your student to dream, to plan, to form relationships, to make an effort, to hang in there—and to celebrate successes.

To Dream. Ask your student to think about the answer to this question: What do you want? What do you really want in life? Encourage him or her to take some time to write down whatever comes to mind. Next, encourage her or him to think about what it would take to get whatever it is that she or he wants. Explain rewards and prices (Lesson 1). Your student can have anything that she or he wants, if she or he is willing to pay the price.

To Plan. Encourage your student to **plan** to get the education or training needed to make those dreams come true.

- What do you need? (money, place to live, child care)

- Where can you get it? (job, housing center, child development center)

- What is required from you? (applications, work, responsibility)

- What help is available? (financial aid, child care, counseling.)

To Form Relationships. Encourage your student to begin to form relationships with people on campus who respect and appreciate him or her. Encourage her or him to begin to make friends with other students, to identify with a peer group, and to be on the lookout for a possible mentor.

To Make an Effort. Encourage your student to **go for it!**

- Attend classes

- Keep up with the homework

- Study for tests

- Keep tutoring appointments

- Keep other commitments

To Hang in There. When the going gets rough, encourage your student to hang in there:

- Take a short break

- Remember your dream

- Visualize your success

- Talk to your mentor

To Celebrate Successes. Don't wait until the end of the semester to celebrate successes! Celebrate getting the homework in on time, celebrate improving on the last quiz, celebrate *every* success. Your taking a few moments to say ''Good job!'' will mean a lot to your student. Soon he or she may begin to notice a lot of successes in his or her life!

What do Tutors Need to Do for Themselves?

1. Keep your boundaries clear. Give only the time and energy to the student that you are comfortable giving. Pay attention to prices that you are and are not willing to pay to be a tutor.

2. Honor yourself for the good work that you do with the student. Give yourself positive messages every day. Avoid punishing yourself, no matter what happens. When the work doesn't go well, reward yourself for your efforts anyway. When the work goes well, celebrate! You deserve it!

3. Get support from other people who value and respect you. Your friends and other tutors may be willing to let you brag when things go well and complain when things go poorly. Do the same for them.

Support Exercise

Name three people on your campus who could be possible mentors for a student at risk.

_____

_____

_____

Name three possible peer groups on your campus for a student at risk.

_____

_____

_____

Healing Opportunity Exercise

Plan a healing experience for a student in the spaces below, using one of the suggestions in this lesson.

Which of the suggested healing opportunities do you plan to arrange?

_____

_____

Who is the student? (Name) _____

Why do you think this experience will be a healing one?

_____

_____

_____

How and when will you carry out this plan?

_____

_____

How will you take care of your own needs?

_____

_____

_____

Evaluation

How did the planned healing experience work out?

_____

_____

What was good about the experience?

_____

_____

What would you do differently next time?

_____

_____

How did you take care of your own needs?

_____

_____

Special Challenges

Tutoring is always a challenge. But sometimes situations arise that require special handling, even for experienced tutors.

As you think about the problems listed below, please remember that no tutor is ever expected to remain in a situation where she or he feels threatened or uncomfortable. You always have the right to end the session or to excuse yourself and go for help. You do not have to be in immediate physical danger to do this. Your feelings are reason enough.

If you feel that you may be in danger, contact your supervisor, contact campus security, or dial 911. Meanwhile try your best to keep the person calm. You might say some comforting things like: ''I'm trying to find a way to help you,'' ''I want to help you,'' ''I'm sorry that this has happened to you.''

If you feel physically threatened, leave the area. You might excuse yourself to go to the restroom, for example, then go to a safe place to call for help. Do not leave the campus unless it is absolutely necessary. When the situation is under control, you may be asked to describe the disturbance to the person in charge.

You may end *any* tutoring session in which you feel uncomfortable. You may end any tutoring relationship *for any reason*. You need only inform your supervisor that you cannot tutor this person any longer. You are not required to explain the reason, although you may do so if you wish.

These cautions are not meant to frighten you. Dangerous situations rarely occur between tutors and tutees. However, a few moments spent thinking about potential problems can make them much easier to solve.

The following real-life situations are presented for your reflection and discussion. There are no right or wrong answers to these problems. The details are purposely vague so that you can imagine the circumstances in your own tutoring experience.

Read the following situations, and imagine yourself in the position of the tutor. *What would you do?* After reflecting on these situations, discuss them with at least one other person. Write down your best solution in the space provided.

1. The tutee is 15-20 minutes late for every group tutoring session. You are getting tired of repeating everything just for him.
   I Would _____
   _____

2. The tutee does not show up for a tutoring session and doesn't call.
   I Would _____
   _____

3. The tutee missed this week's session. Now she is desparate for help. She wants you to tutor her during your lunch break.
   I Would _____
   _____

4. Instead of listening, this tutee tries to tell you how the work should be done.
   I Would _____
   _____

5. The tutee criticizes the instructor of the course, a person you respect.
   I Would _____
   _____

6. The tutee criticizes the instructor of the course, and frankly, you have some reservations about this instructor yourself.
   I Would _____
   _____

7. A tutee makes sexually suggestive remarks, which you dislike.
   I Would _____
   _____

8. The tutee has unpleasant body odor.
   I Would _____
   _____

9. The tutee frequently uses language that is offensive to you.

I Would _____

_____

10. The tutee is behaving in a very strange way today. You feel uncomfortable.

I Would _____

_____

11. The tutee appears to be drunk.

I Would _____

_____

12. The tutee becomes very sad and tearful during a session.

I Would _____

_____

13. The tutee is extremely worried about low grades. He hints that he is considering suicide.

I Would _____

_____

14. You are afraid of a tutee who has threatened to harm you.

I Would _____

_____

15. You are afraid of a tutee, although you are not sure why.

I Would _____

_____

16. A tutee expects you to edit her papers on demand.

I Would _____

_____

17. The tutee brings you an expensive gift, which you know he cannot afford.

I Would _____

_____

18. The tutee desperately needs a place to live.

I Would _____

_____

19. The tutee is falling behind because she is exhausted from work, school, and family obligations.

I Would _____

_____

20. The tutee desperately needs money. You have a few dollars that you could spare.

I Would _____

_____

NOTES

NOTES

FOR OTHER FIFTY-MINUTE SELF-STUDY BOOKS
SEE THE BACK OF THIS BOOK.

NOTES

FOR OTHER FIFTY-MINUTE SELF-STUDY BOOKS
SEE THE BACK OF THIS BOOK.

NOTES

FOR OTHER FIFTY-MINUTE SELF-STUDY BOOKS
SEE THE BACK OF THIS BOOK.

ABOUT THE FIFTY-MINUTE SERIES

We hope you enjoyed this book and found it valuable. If so, we have good news for you. This title is part of the best selling *FIFTY-MINUTE Series* of books. All other books are similar in size and identical in price. Several books are supported with a training video. These are identified by the symbol **V** next to the title.

Since the first *FIFTY-MINUTE* book appeared in 1986, more than five million copies have been sold worldwide. Each book was developed with the reader in mind. The result is a concise, high quality module written in a positive, readable self-study format.

FIFTY-MINUTE Books and Videos are available from your distributor or from Crisp Publications, Inc., 95 First Street, Los Altos, CA 94022. A free current catalog is available on request.

The complete list of *FIFTY-MINUTE Series* Books and Videos are listed on the following pages and organized by general subject area.

MANAGEMENT TRAINING (Cont.)

PERSONNEL/HUMAN RESOURCES

COMMUNICATIONS

CUSTOMER SERVICE/SALES TRAINING (CONT.)

SMALL BUSINESS/FINANCIAL PLANNING

ADULT LITERACY/BASIC LEARNING

CAREER BUILDING